# For Inshriach

First published in Great Britain in 2009 and the USA in 2010 by
Frances Lincoln Children's Books, 4 Torriano Mews,
Torriano Avenue, London NW5 2RZ
www.franceslincoln.com

PHOTOGRAPHIC ACKNOWLEDGEMENTS
Please note: the pages in this book are not numbered. The text begins on page 6
Cover & pages 16/17: © The National Gallery, London
Pages 6/7: Museum of Modern Art, New York (Mrs Simon Guggenheim Fund. 146.1945), © ADAGP, Paris and DACS, London 2009.
Digital image © 2008 The Museum of Modern Art/Scala, Florence
Pages 8/9:  The J. Paul Getty Museum, Los Angeles
Pages 10/11: Museum of Modern Art, New York (Gift of Joachim Aberbach [by exchange]. 229.1988), © ADAGP, Paris and DACS, London 2009.
Digital image © 2008 The Museum of Modern Art/Scala, Florence
Pages 12/13: Tate, London, © Peter Blake. All rights reserved, DACS, London 2009. Digital image © Tate, London 2009
Pages 14/15: The Escorial, Prado, Madrid. Photo © 1995 Scala, Florence
Pages 18/19: Tate, London. Digital image © Tate, London 2009
Pages 20/21: © The National Gallery, London
Pages 22/23: The J. Paul Getty Museum, Los Angeles
Pages 24/25: © V&A Images, Victoria and Albert Museum
All rights reserved

British Library Cataloguing in Publication Data
available on request

ISBN: 978-1-84507-636-8

Set in Stone Sans and Felt Tip

Printed in China
1 3 5 7 9 8 6 4 2

# In the PICTURE

Here are 10 specially chosen pictures, all from the world's great art museums. Look at them closely. Think about what you see and how they make you feel. There are details to find, questions to answer and lots more besides...

## Lucy Micklethwait

F
FRANCES LINCOLN
CHILDREN'S BOOKS

# WHAT'S IN THE PICTURE?
## Here are six close-ups – can you find them in the painting opposite?

- Can you find two upside-down houses and an upside-down lady?

- Do you think the green man speaks English?

- Does he have a low voice, a gentle voice, a high voice or a squeaky voice?

- How does the upside-down lady sound when she speaks?

## I and the Village, 1911
*Marc Chagall, 1887-1985*

Chagall was living in Paris when he painted this picture, but he was thinking about the country town in Russia where he grew up. On farms, people and animals depend on one another – notice how the green man and the cow are staring into each other's eyes as if they were best friends. The painting is like a dream where nothing quite makes sense, so we can decide for ourselves what the artist is trying to say.

## JUST FOR FUN

Make up a conversation between the green man and the cow.

Use details in the painting to give you ideas.

# Parrots, a horse, a camel and more – can you find them in the picture opposite?

## The Entry of the Animals into Noah's Ark, 1613
*Jan Brueghel the Elder, 1568-1625*

God told Noah that a great flood was coming to wipe out all the wicked people in the world. He told Noah to take his family and two of every animal, one male and one female, on board a wooden boat called the Ark, to save them from being drowned. In this picture the Ark is a long way away and all the animals are being herded towards it. Do you think they will get there in time?

- Can you find lions and leopards in the painting?

- Can you find two porcupines, two guinea pigs and two turtles?

- Can you find two monkeys?

- What a lot of birds! How many can you count?

**JUST FOR FUN**
Write a list of all the animals in the picture.
Tick the ones which you have seen in real life.

## 122 RUE DU TEMPLE, 1968
*Jacques Mahé de la Villeglé, born 1926*

The artist found a wall covered in layers of torn posters in a street in Paris. He lifted this huge section and stuck it on to a piece of linen. This type of art is called 'décollage', the opposite of 'collage'. He says that all the unknown people who ripped the paper away when it was on the wall are artists too. The name of the street was Rue du Temple which he used as the title.

# These details belong somewhere in the torn picture – but where?

- How many faces can you find?
- Is anybody speaking?
- Find the date '1968'.
- Find the word 'PARISIENS'.

## JUST FOR FUN

Make your own décollage. Pull out five spreads from the middle of a magazine. Paste the first on to a piece of card using glue. Stick on the remaining pages, one on top of the other, as if you were sticking posters to a billboard. Leave to dry for a few minutes. Rip off bits wherever you like. Choose the section of your billboard which you like the best and cut it out to display.

# Paintbrushes, a dog, model toys and more belong somewhere in the window opposite - but where?

- Find the number 31. Why is it there?

- How many ways of getting about can you find?

- How many flags can you see?

- If you could buy just one thing from this store, what would it be?

**The Toy Shop, 1962**
*Peter Blake, born 1932*

Peter Blake loves collecting things. For him, this is not only a work of art but a store for his collection of toys. The shop front looks flat in this book, but in fact the door is a real wooden door, the glass is real, and all the toys and pictures are real too.

## JUST FOR FUN

Make a collage of a window like this. It could be displaying sweets,
perhaps, or junk. Find a piece of cardboard, then look through magazines
and cut out pictures of things that you would like to sell. Stick them on
the cardboard. Finally, cut narrow strips of coloured paper to make the
bars across the windows, and slightly wider strips for the window-frame.

## JUST FOR FUN

Paint or draw a picture of demons. They could be partly human,
partly animal or partly machine.

# Find these strange details in the even stranger painting.

- Beside the pig there is a mischievous demon. What is it going to do?

- A face is looking out of the water at St Anthony. What do you think it is saying?

- What are the demons behind the tree doing?

- The branches of the tree are dead. What animal's head do they remind you of?

## The Temptations of St Anthony
*Hieronymus Bosch, about 1450-1516*

Saint Anthony was a monk, a holy man. He is sitting under a tree with his faithful pig, trying to pray. All around him there are demons and half-human creatures trying to tempt him away from his prayers and lead him astray. Do you think he is listening to them? On his cloak is the Greek letter 'tau', a symbol adopted by the Christian Church.

- How many hats can you find in the painting?

- Do you think the water is warm or cold? Why?

- Is anybody talking?

- Can you find the artist's signature?

**JUST FOR FUN**

Take a piece of paper, preferably coloured. Cut out lots of people
from a magazine. They can be whole or in parts. Arrange them
on the paper however you like and stick them on. Make up a story
about the people you have chosen.

# Everyone's having a good rest – can you find these close-ups in the painting?

## Bathers at Asnières, 1884
*Georges Seurat, 1859-1891*

The town of Asnières is near Paris on the bank of the River Seine. It is an industrial town with many factories. These young men are factory workers taking a break, probably in their lunch hour. The boy sitting on the bank looks as if he has been working very hard. Crossing the river is a passenger boat on its way to the island in the river. The real picture is enormous. Seurat went out and made many small sketches of real people before deciding where to place them on the canvas, when he was back in his studio.

# Find these six details on the board opposite.

- Can you find the artist's name?

- How many objects are tucked into each band of leather?

- Can you find a stick of sealing wax? What are the red blobs on the back of the envelope?

- Can you find a quill pen and a penknife? What do you think the penknife was used for?

**A Trompe l'Oeil of Newspapers, Letters and Writing Implements on a Wooden Board, about 1699**
*Edward Collier, active 1662-1708*

If you saw this painting hanging on the wall, you might think that the letters and objects tucked into the ribbon were real. That is what the artist wants you to think. This sort of painting was very fashionable when Edward Collier was alive, and he painted lots of them. It is called a 'trompe l'oeil' which means 'tricks the eye'.

## JUST FOR FUN

Make your own letter-board. Find a piece of cardboard, not too thick. Glue on to it a piece of textured material (felt is good) and cut away the edges. Cut 2 pieces of strong tape to make the straps. Make holes with a skewer in the positions where the brass paper fasteners will go (ask an adult to help here). Push the fasteners through to the back and open them out. Punch holes in the top edge and thread a piece of ribbon through the board to hang it up.

## JUST FOR FUN

Imagine that you have a special angel to look after you. What would your angel look like? What would he or she be called? What would his or her wings be made of? Draw or paint a picture of your own guardian angel.

# These close-ups all belong in the angel painting – but where?

- Can you find a dog?

- What is Tobias wearing? Describe his clothes.

- Look for two hands which are almost the same.

- How would you describe the angel's wings?

**Tobias and the Angel, 1470-80**
*Workshop of Andrea del Verrocchio*

Tobias is on his way home carrying a fish he has caught. The insides of the fish will be used as medicine to cure his father's blindness. Travelling with him is the Archangel Raphael who is protecting him and looking after the precious medicine in a little round box.

## JUST FOR FUN
Look around the room you are in and find one object to draw
(a cup perhaps, a shoe, even a violin). Look hard at it and
draw it as many times as you like, in different colours.

# Find where these six close-ups belong in the crowded artist's studio.

- Can you find a flying baby and a plaster foot?

- What do you think is inside the trunk?

- How many musical instruments can you find?

- Where is the skull?

**The Drawing Lesson, about 1665**
*Jan Steen, 1626-1679*

All is quiet in the studio except for the scratching of the artist's pen.
He is concentrating on his drawing while his two pupils watch.
Today he seems to be using the figure of a nude man for the lesson
but there are lots of other things in the studio to draw.

# This battle scene is busy, busy, busy – can you work out where the details fit?

- How many warriors and horses can you find?
- What weapons are the soldiers using?
- The soldiers are riding horses. Can you find another kind of animal in the picture?

## The Battle of Bundi (about 1590s), from the Akbarnama
*Tulsi the Elder*

This painting is one of the many illustrations to the *Akbarnama*, the story of the life of the great Mughal emperor Akbar. Bundi (in Rajastan, India) was one of the many cities he captured during his reign. You can see it in the top left corner. Akbar was interested in painting and set up studios which employed skilled local artists.

JUST FOR FUN
Look at the rich patterns in the picture opposite. Use them to inspire your own pattern-picture. Draw some lines or squiggles on a piece of white paper. Fill in the spaces with patterns (spots, stripes or criss-cross, perhaps) in different colours.

# GET LOOKING, GET THINKING
## Can you name these creatures?

## What shapes can you find in the details below?

# Make up names for these strange creatures.

# Design your own battledress using these patterns.

# What colours can you see in the details below?

Look hard at one of the window panes below for one minute. Now look away and write down every object you can remember.

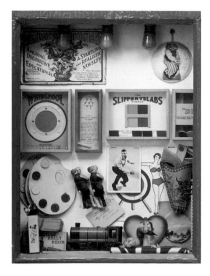

In each column below, the detail at the top belongs in the same picture as one of the three details below it. Which one of the three?